THE CALL

THE CALL

Finding your way on the
journey to full-time ministry

Trevor Archer
and Paul Mallard

10 Publishing
a division of 10 of those.com

First published in Great Britain in 2016

British Library Cataloguing in Publication Data
A record for this book is available from the British Library

ISBN: 978-1-910587-50-8

Designed by Diane Warnes

Printed in the UK by CPI

10Publishing, a division of 10ofthose.com
Unit C, Tomlinson Road, Leyland, PR25 2DY, England
Email: info@10ofthose.com
Website: www.10ofthose.com

CONTENTS

INTRODUCTION

The Hub Conference was launched by the Fellowship of Independent Evangelical Churches (FIEC) as an annual conference to help men and women find clear routes into independent church ministry. For those 'just looking' as well as those 'just started', 'The Hub' supports and equips them in their journey through training and into gospel ministry.

Led by experienced gospel workers from the FIEC, and supported by leaders from colleges and courses, The Hub Conference provides Bible ministry and a wide range of seminars on ministry-related issues. Out of that conference this series of books was born. It's designed to resource people in many areas of Christian work and for a lifetime of ministry.

Someone once described theological books as 'a "college of teachers" committed to helping you do your best to handle the Word of truth'. We hope this series will play a small but significant part in that library of wisdom, at whatever stage you find yourself.

We hope that these books will also be a great help to pastors and leaders, not only in providing a refresher, but also to equip those you are discipling in your congregation for leadership and ministry.

This book, written by Paul Mallard and Trevor Archer, simply aims too provide a basic introduction into the subject of how men and women might discern and then map their route into paid Christian ministry. Whilst written with an independent church context in mind, the principles here are transferable into other church groupings.

This is not a comprehensive 'how to' guide and it is certainly not a definitive answer to all the questions that arise when considering the call to ministry! There are many variations on a theme by which the Lord might bring a person into gospel ministry, the permutations of which cannot possibly be covered in one book, whatever its size. Everyone now in Christian ministry will have their own story to tell of how their personal journey unfolded.

Paul Mallard was converted at the age of eleven and as early as only fourteen years of age had a strangely compelling sense that God was calling him into some form of Christian ministry. This sense of call determined his choice of A levels and the university course he studied. He was advised by a visiting preacher: 'Go and get a proper job before going into ministry!' Therefore Paul became a teacher. However, throughout his short teaching career, the conviction that he was to spend his life teaching the Bible did not go away. At the age of twenty-five, he became an elder of his local church and in only the following year, 1982, Paul found himself pastoring the church! He has been in pastoral ministry ever since.

Trevor Archer, on the other hand, came into ministry through quite a different route. Leaving school at sixteen, he trained as a chartered surveyor and had become a partner in a London practice when, in his early thirties, he sensed God's call to go into gospel ministry. In 1986 he found himself co-pastoring the very church he had been converted in during his late teens.

The point is that every story is unique. Nevertheless, certain features remain consistent throughout: the need for conversion, for inner conviction, for a desire to serve God, for a proven character, for the appropriate gift and for the approval of godly leaders and God's people. Woven into all these things will be the strangely wonderful providences of God.

What follows is the unpacking of some of the basic biblical principles and biblical wisdom that have a bearing on the issues of the call and ways into Christian ministry. We want to help a range of people. You may be at the beginning of the process and are 'just looking' into it, or you may be at the end of the process and simply want some confirmation of your calling.

We hope that for some of you this book will confirm you in your convictions that God is calling you to ministry. However, for others it might help you to recognise that it is not the right way to go. Either outcome will mean that the book has done its job. May the Lord use this book to help you on your journey.

Trevor Archer and Paul Mallard

fiec

the FELLOWSHIP of INDEPENDENT EVANGELICAL CHURCHES

THE CALL TO MINISTRY

In recent decades the topic of 'the call' to ministry has been a topic of some controversy and confusion.[1] At one extreme is the view that places great weight and store on the individual's subjective experience of a clear 'call' as a prerequisite to ministry. This would usually anticipate a clear and discernible 'God has called me' element or experience. In reaction to this tradition, which has sometimes led to patently unsuitable folk putting themselves forward for ministry, an approach gained favour which majored instead upon the objective that 'as long as the person has a proven character and a proven gift and wants to go into ministry, they are called'.

The Bible is far more nuanced. God's call will involve subjective factors, not least a growing inner conviction and desire to serve. As Paul puts it in 1 Timothy 3:1: '*whoever aspires to be an overseer desires a noble task*'. This is obviously personal and subjective. At the same time this personal aspiration must be coupled to and recognised objectively by the church. So verse 2 continues: '*the overseer is to be above reproach, faithful to his wife, temperate, self-controlled, respectable, hospitable, able to teach*'. These are all very objective and clearly visible traits!

The Lord may well use various ways and means to provide a person with an inner conviction and compulsion, in which every story is different and every sense of call unique. But such a sense of personal 'call' is never divorced from the objective evidence to be sought in the life and character of that person. In this manner the Bible encourages us to look for the glorious blend of both aspects, signalling a suitability for Christian ministry.

There is therefore nothing 'super-spiritual' or 'mystical' here – rather a wonderful biblical realism and bringing together of the subjective and the objective, of personal as well as public recognition. God sets the bar high whilst affirming that He calls imperfect people to serve Him, empowered by His grace – as the Apostle Paul readily testified: the Lord *'said to me, "My grace is sufficient for you, for my power is made perfect in weakness"'* (2 Cor. 12:9).

Christ is passionate about His church and He is the one who gives spiritual gifts to His Bride (Eph. 4:7–16). He has determined that healthy leadership and workers are vital to the spiritual well-being of His church and the spread of the gospel. It is He who calls us to service and He will make His way clear. He will direct our paths. It is our duty to trust and obey (Prov. 3:5–6).

Given that every Christian is called to serve (Eph. 2:10; 2 Cor. 5:14–15), what 'marks' are we to look for in anyone who feels called to a 'full-time' Christian ministry? Whether it be as a pastor, evangelist, church planter, women's worker, children's or youth minister or in overseas mission, what are the 'marks' that give confidence to both the person and the church that the 'call' is authentic and of God?

Here are twelve important marks to look for. It is important to remember that God is not looking for perfection and that none of these will be seen in full bloom! However, at the same time there ought to be, however embryonic, some evidence of each of the following (not least the first mark!):

TWELVE MARKS TO LOOK FOR IN A PERSON CALLED TO GOSPEL MINISTRY

1. A Christian

This may seem a 'given', and such an obvious point as to be an unnecessary place to start! Until, that is, we remind ourselves that it is tragically perfectly possible for someone to claim to be sent from God but prove to be a false prophet, a wolf in sheep's clothing. It is not only contemporary denominations that are riddled with unsaved, unbelieving leaders; the frightening fact is that the evangelical scene is not exempt from the danger.

When the Bible talks about calling it is usually referring to the call to salvation rather than the call to ministry. The effectual call is that direct summons which comes from God through human agencies and which raises us from spiritual death and brings us into fellowship with Jesus (1 Cor. 1:9; Rom. 8:30; 2 Thes. 2:13–14). This call to salvation must precede the call to ministry. Sometimes unconverted men become pastor-teachers, which inevitably proves to be a disaster for them and for the church.

In his book *The Reformed Pastor,* Richard Baxter warns: 'Take heed to yourselves least you should be void of that saving grace of God which you offer to others, and be strangers to the effectual working of that gospel which you preach ... Take heed to yourselves, lest you perish while you call upon others to take heed to perishing.'[2] Spurgeon put it like this: 'A graceless pastor is a blind man elected to a professorship of optics. He is a dumb man elevated to the chair of music.'[3]

2. A love for Jesus

When Jesus called Peter to shepherd His flock, He first questioned him over the depths of his devotion: *'do you love me?'* (John 21:15–17). Ministry flows out of a love for Jesus. The Lord's criticism of the church in Ephesus was that whilst it was sound and busy and persevering and faithful, it had deserted its *'first love'* (Rev. 2:1–7 NKJV).

The greatest challenge in gospel ministry is to ensure that Jesus has His rightful place in our lives. The greatest danger in ministry is to allow other things to take His place. It is a terrible reality but often the main obstacle to loving God is the service of God! It is a frightening truth but it is quite possible for a person to be in 'love' with a particular ministry or status in the church rather than in love with the Lord.

It is being 'in Christ' alone which gives the Christian their identity and worth, not our work for him and certainly not the 'status' any ministry gives. Long after any ministry is taken from a Christian by time or circumstance, it is this identity 'in Christ' which remains. So when considering a valid call to ministry here are some vital questions to ask:

- Is there a delight and intimacy in a relationship with the Father?
- Is there a sense of being captivated with Jesus? (How can you proclaim a captivating Saviour if not captivated with Jesus?)
- Is there a sensitivity to the voice of the Spirit in the Word?

This may sound rather subjective but if a person is not daily devoted to Jesus, to pleasing Him and to being soaked in His Word and ways, they will not survive the rigours of ministry. They will eventually either lapse into bitterness and cynicism or bail out. Thus a person's devotional life, which feeds and expresses devotion to Christ, is very important. It will not suddenly improve once someone enters paid ministry. Unless healthy patterns already exist they are unlikely to develop later.

George Müller wrote: 'I saw more clearly than ever that the first great and primary business to which I ought to attend every day was, to have my soul happy in the Lord ... How different [each day was] when the soul is refreshed and made happy early in the morning.' A regular pattern of a personal prayer life, of feeding on God's Word on a daily basis and of bringing Him praise is the fuel that sustains ministry.

3. A love for God's Word

All Christian ministry, whether preaching, pastoring or evangelism, or cross-cultural, children's, youth or women's work, has at its heart understanding, teaching, applying and living out the gospel in all its breadth and depth.

A call to ministry will therefore entail a constant appetite to get to grips with the Bible, to understand the unfolding story of salvation from Genesis to Revelation, and to handle the Word of God in a biblical manner in order to apply it correctly. This is a lifetime activity – nobody ever 'arrives' in this regard – for there is always more truth and wisdom to be mined from the Word of God and brought to bear on life. So it is important that there is evidence in the life of anyone aspiring to ministry that there is a love for and growing understanding of the Word of God, a rejoicing in the gospel, a delight with its glory, and an excitement about its power.

This is not saying that a person must have an

'academic' bent or theological qualifications – some may, but that in itself is not a qualification. What matters is an appetite for God's Word, a readiness to get to grips with the great doctrines of the faith, and a hunger to understand how the gospel applies to all of life in all its complexity, challenges and issues. All ministry in this regard is Word ministry for it flows from the bedrock of the Bible properly understood and applied.

4. A love for God's people

Jesus obviously loves the church – He gave Himself up for her (Eph. 5:25). She is His reward (John 17:6, 24) and she is destined for glory (Eph. 5:26–27). A call to a ministry that in any way belittles or effectively bypasses the local church is not in line with God's Big Story!

Richard Baxter, commenting on the pastorate, put it like this: 'The pastor needs to delight in the beauty of the church, long for its happiness, seek for its good and rejoice in its welfare. He must be willing to spend and be spent for the church.'[4] Church, of course, means the people who make up the church of the living God. If the local church does not have a high place in a person's mind and heart, if they are not already dedicated to serving the church, then any such 'call' is very questionable!

Christopher Ash, Director of the Cornhill Training Course, has helped train hundreds of men and women for ministry. When asked what he looks for in any 'call to ministry', he replied: 'What I increasingly want to know of men and women aspiring to go into Christian work is this: Do they love people?'

And this, of course, is where the reality check kicks in. Whilst people who make up the church can be delightful, enchanting and encouraging, they can also be frustrating, difficult and stubborn. It is tempting to think of ministry in romantic terms without facing the reality of real people with real problems! As one wag once put it: 'Church would be great if it wasn't for the people!'

Never think of gospel ministry in a vacuum. Some people in church are 'grace growers'. That might sound great but actually these are the people who are so difficult that God uses them to grow the grace of patience and compassion in our lives! A call to ministry of whatever kind is a call to love and serve people.

In 1 Thessalonians 2 Paul uses intimate imagery to describe the nature of his ministry among the young church there in Thessalonica: *'Just as a nursing mother cares for her children, so we cared for you. Because we loved you so much, we were delighted to share with you not only the gospel of God but our lives as well'* (vv. 7–8).

A heart to be around people, a willingness to share life with others, a readiness to face conflict resolution for the sake of the gospel, and the capacity to maintain a thick skin with a tender heart – these are all marks of Christian love.

5. A love for the lost

Ministry of whatever kind will have at its core a desire to see people come to Christ and thus be rescued from the wrath to come. Therefore any sense of a call to ministry will have at its heart a desire to see lost people saved. This is particularly pertinent to those who aspire to a preaching ministry, to evangelism or to cross-cultural work. A heart for the lost is not something magically endowed once a person has been commissioned to a ministry; it has to be part of who they are and how they 'tick'. So questions about the number of non-Christian friends a person has, the consistency with which they pray for unbelievers and their readiness to witness to unbelievers provide the best answers to this aspect of any call.

Those aspiring to pastoral ministry are often far more comfortable feeding sheep than fishing for men! Jesus did both. One of the common criticisms Jesus faced was that He spent too much time with sinners. He associated with the unwelcome and rejected. How many of us could be accused of spending too much time with 'outcasts'? In Luke 19:10 Jesus says that He came to seek and save the lost. This same Jesus says to us: *'As the Father has sent me, I am sending you'* (John 20:21).

6. A desire to serve

The Christian model of leadership is radically different to that which the world aspires to and promotes. In God's kingdom, the least is the greatest; the most heroic is the one who is servant of all.

God does not call a man or woman to that which they are not already doing in this regard. A call to ministry is essentially a call to serve God, His gospel, His people and His world. Paul says that one of the qualifications for eldership is a desire to want to do the job: *'Here is a trustworthy saying: whoever aspires to be an overseer desires a noble task'* (1 Tim. 3:1). The word translated 'aspires' means 'to stretch oneself out in order to touch or grasp something'. It is to 'desire passionately'.

It is not ungodly to want to serve God's kingdom – quite the opposite, in fact!

It is right to expect that there should be some level of longing and desire. Naturally it will be coupled to a sense of inadequacy – that's no bad thing! Even so, there should be present some legitimate God-given ambition to serve.

Such a desire will be evidenced by an awareness and readiness that sees what needs to be done and sets about the task. It will find expression in different ways in different personality types. Whilst a desire to serve is not enough in itself and needs to be accompanied by other criteria, an absence of such desire or reluctance to serve ought to ring alarm bells.

7. A maturing character

The qualifications for Christian ministry are essentially the same as those required for overseers (also known as elders), as set out in 1 Timothy 3:2–7 (below). The striking thing about this passage is that it is essentially all about character; indeed, this is a character reference rather than a job description!

> **Now the overseer is to be above reproach, faithful to his wife, temperate, self-controlled, respectable, hospitable, able to teach, not given to drunkenness, not violent but gentle, not quarrelsome, not a lover of money. He must manage his own family well and see that his children obey him, and he must do so in a manner worthy of full respect. (If anyone does not know how to manage his own family, how can he take care of God's church?) He must not be a recent convert, or he may become conceited and fall under the same judgment as the devil. He must also have a good reputation with outsiders, so that he will not fall into disgrace and into the devil's trap.**

Those to be appointed to leadership in the church are to be blameless and above reproach, and mature in their faith rather than being a new convert. The parallel list in Titus 1:6–9 makes the same point.

The Bible always places character before gifting. Why? Because you can and should always work hard at developing the gift(s) God has given you, but if there is a fundamental flaw in your character, it will undermine and eventually destroy any ministry, however gifted.

Ministry exists in the context of character. Character authenticates leadership. Robert Murray M'Cheyne captured it when he said: 'It is not great gifts that God blesses so much as great likeness to Christ. The greatest need of my people is my own personal holiness.'

It is important to remember this is not a description of sinless perfection – if that were the case, there would be no Christian workers! Every Christian struggles with sin (Rom. 7:21–24), every Christian needs forgiveness (1 John 1:8 – 2:2) and every Christian is a sinner saved by grace who ministers to other sinners saved by grace. There is no special experience that lifts those working in Christian ministry into a new sphere of flawless holiness.

At the same time the very 'ordinariness' of the characteristics listed in the pastoral epistles are simply highlighting what is to be the 'normal' life expected of a Christian, regardless of whether they aspire to paid ministry or not. So let's be clear: we are not talking here about a uniquely holy and singularly one-off brand of Christian who is thus suited to ministry. Rather, anyone aspiring to Christian ministry should simply evidence the character of a maturing Christian, growing in the grace and love of Christ. (Note my wording of a 'maturing' Christian, not a 'mature' Christian, since every follower of Christ is a work in progress, a work that continues until the day of home calling!)

Kevin DeYoung puts it like this:

> My congregation needs me to be humble before they need me to be smart. They need me to be honest more than they need me to be a dynamic leader. They need me to be teachable more than they need me to teach at conferences. If your walk matches your talk, if your faith costs you something, if being a Christian is more than a cultural garb, they will listen to you.[5]

So when considering a call to ministry, or helping evaluate one, take a long hard look at the qualifications set out in the pastoral epistles and ask are there areas that need to be worked on, is there evidence of the Holy Spirit at work and is there growing likeness to Christ?

8. A stability in relationships

Contrary to popular perception in some quarters, being married is not an essential qualification for ministry! Indeed, unmarried men and women have made an immense contribution to the work of mission and the growth of the church throughout 2,000 years of church history. The Apostle Paul is but one example (1 Cor. 7:7)! At the same time married men and women have formed strong units in ministry that have greatly blessed the cause of the gospel.

So when it comes to the question of 'call', don't just focus on whether a person is married or not, and how that affects their suitability for ministry. A man or woman who is single when first responding to the call to ministry might find themselves married five, ten or even twenty years later! Conversely a married couple entering ministry might experience a bereavement that leaves the spouse single.

Rather, when examining a person's suitability for ministry, it is far better and more helpful to look at this issue in terms of the stability and appropriateness of their relationships, particularly with the opposite sex. Consider again those qualifications for eldership in 1 Timothy 3, but this time with the two particular references to marriage removed. It is striking how relational the qualities are that are to be evidenced in a leader. Qualities such as humility, respect, appropriateness, purity, consistency and other-person centredness are high on the list of the Bible's qualifications for role modelling good relationships.

Of course, if a person is married any consideration of a call must be done in the context of the health of their marriage. It does not have to be perfect (surprisingly perhaps such a marriage does not exist!) but there should be clear evidence of faithfulness and love which mirrors in some measure the love that Christ has for His church (1 Tim. 3:2; Eph. 5:25–33).

Furthermore the spouse must be supportive of the call to ministry of their partner. Inevitably Christian ministry will have implications for a marriage and a family. There will be particular burdens to bear and pressures to withstand which a call to ministry will impose. There will be a certain loss of privacy, the challenge of difficult people and an emotional cost to be paid. Unless both in the marriage are committed to the call it will not work. These things must be fully discussed and explored.

9. A teachable spirit

The greatest challenge anybody faces in Christian ministry is themselves! So it is important that a man or woman considering a call to ministry has a self-awareness that invites other Christians to speak into their lives and welcomes constructive critique of their character and abilities. The attitude needed can be summed up in one word: 'teachability'.

The New Testament is replete with actions to 'one another'. For example, in Ephesians we read we should be *'bearing with one another in love'* (4:2); *'Be kind and compassionate to one another, forgiving each other'* (4:32); and be *'speaking to one another with psalms, hymns, and songs'* (5:19). Given this, is there evidence of a humble and teachable spirit that invites other Christians to speak the truth in love into their life?

Self-awareness is shown in an ability to identify one's own strengths and weaknesses, coupled to some degree with an emotional intelligence that welcomes trusted friends to challenge and if needs be rebuke them for the sake of the gospel. A prickly, easily affronted and angered individual might be very gifted and convinced of God's call upon their life – but they are seriously mistaken! Pride will indeed go before a fall. If a person cannot laugh at themselves in this regard it is never a good sign that they will thrive in ministry, where a sense of humour is a wonderful release valve and essential to good emotional health!

A man or woman whom God is calling to serve Him knows something of their pride being subdued (1 Pet. 5:5) and their lives being shaped by some experience of 'brokenness'. All of this enables them to realise that God is moulding and teaching them through such experiences, and creating a humble dependence upon Him that invites the counsel of wise friends.

10. A giftedness for the task

This may seem, and indeed it is, a pretty obvious thing to mention but it is one that needs saying, given that it is possible for a person to convince themselves of their giftedness in a particular area of ministry when none actually exists!

Take for instance a man who might love to study and pore over the Bible. He may well do this out of a genuine heart and passion for God's Word. His intellectual capacity means that he has a really good grasp of theology and doctrine. He finds it a pleasure to dig into the Scriptures and he is diligent and earnest in the task.

Yet when put in front of a congregation, though 'solid' in his doctrine and use of the Bible, he is totally lacking in any real ability to communicate. In fact he comes across as rather dull and boring – and worse still makes the Bible seem dull and boring! Furthermore, he seems to have lost sight that real people with real problems are in front of him! Simply put, he is not gifted for the task of a pastor-preacher.

That is because preaching is not just 'giving a talk'; it demands giftedness. As Bruce Thielman puts it: 'The pulpit calls those anointed to it as the sea calls its sailors. And like the sea it batters and bruises and does not rest. To preach, to really preach, is to die naked a little at a time, and to know each time you do it that you're going to have to do it again.'[6]

The pastor must have the ability not only to teach God's Word (1 Tim. 3:2) but to feed the sheep (John 21:17). In what amounts to Paul's final counsel to Timothy in his last letter he says: '*In the presence of God and of Christ Jesus, who will judge the living and the dead, and in view of his appearing and his kingdom, I give you this charge*' (2 Tim. 4:1).

This is really important – really, really, really important! What moves Paul to such an extravagant use of language? He tells us in the next verse: '*preach the word*'. A pastor needs the ability and gifting to be able to feed his congregation on a regular basis and connect and apply the gospel into the mess which is our everyday life.

11. An evidence of God's blessing

Coupled to this issue of giftedness comes a question that is seldom asked of those aspiring to ministry. What evidence is there that the Lord has used you to bless others in the area of ministry to which you feel called? It is an entirely legitimate and important question.

For those aspiring to be an evangelist, where is the evidence of God's blessing in terms of people helped to Christ through them? For those convinced of God's call to go into overseas mission, where is the evidence that the Lord has used them in their home country to connect with and bring people from other nationalities, languages and cultures to Christ? You get the point!

The subjective needs to be tested by the objective. This is where the local church comes in. A call comes from God through the medium of the church. Charles Bridges put it like this: 'The external call is a commission received from and recognised by the Church ... not qualifying the Minister, but accrediting him'[7]. Charles Spurgeon made the same point: 'The will of the Lord concerning pastors is made known through the prayerful judgment of the church. It is needful as a proof of your vocation that your preaching is acceptable to the people of God.'[8]

This is why the role of the local church and, in particular, local church leaders is integral in this matter of calling. It is the role of church leaders to be on the lookout for where the Lord is at work in the church. It is the leaders and the church who are to be in the vanguard when it comes to recognising God's call on a person's life. It is part of their job to identify, test, equip and mobilise new leaders (2 Tim. 2:2).

And that calls for a solemn, serious and prayerful consideration of the biblical criteria, to be confident that both character and competence are present in the one called. Has the Lord gifted and equipped the person for the task they are called to? Reaching a decision requires a partnership between the church and the individual. The church must be on the lookout for those with a calling, and the individual open and submissive to the wisdom of the church.

12. The 3 G's – grace, grit and gumption

First, just as the Christian life is grace from first to last, so too for anyone to stay the course in Christian ministry will require grace from first to last. As Newton put it in his famous hymn 'Amazing Grace': 'and grace will lead me home'. It is by God's grace that He entrusts His work to frail and fallible human beings, and it is only grace that will enable anyone to survive and thrive in ministry and reach the finishing line.

But, secondly, ministry also needs grit. It is demanding and there is a measure of sacrifice involved. Paul speaks of the sufferings he endured for the church (2 Cor. 4:4–12). God poured suffering into Paul's life so that He could then pour in His comfort – a comfort that would then flow out of Paul into the lives of others (2 Cor. 1:3–11).

In some mysterious way his suffering was filling up what was missing from Christ's suffering (Col. 1:24). The test of any Christian worker is their willingness to lay down their life for the flock (John 10:11, 15, 17). It requires a God-given grit that will enable a person to marshal their resources to serve God faithfully for as long as possible.

Thirdly, ministry will require gumption. Gumption is the ability to decide what is the best thing to do in a particular situation, and to do it with energy and determination. Shepherds are called to lead the flock forward (1 Pet. 5:1–4) and this will involve the management of necessary biblical change. One of the central tasks of any Christian leader is to influence God's people towards God's purposes, moving them towards God's agenda.

These 3 G's must be present now in some measure, however formative. Are there signs of perseverance in grace, of stickability and of leadership in the person's life and service? If so, it should give some good confidence in regards to a 'call'.

WHAT NEXT?

A certain older generation was brought up on the mantra: 'Do not enter the ministry if you can help it'! As a result many were put off course for a while until a little reflection caused them to question whether this was really biblical advice. Certainly a person should not consider ministry until they have counted the cost. However, many men and women have testified that in the end they were left with no choice – they had a growing conviction that going into ministry was God's will. Those same people would also identify with the twelve marks described above.

These twelve marks are not an exhaustive list – though having read them you may feel exhausted! To reiterate the point made at the outset, they are not intended to daunt or disqualify but rather provide a good start and reference point for those considering, or helping folk consider, whether God is calling them to a ministry.

Where do you go from here? In the next section, on the ways into ministry, some pointers are given for those for whom the sense of call has been confirmed and encouraged. But before that it may well be appropriate for some who are considering ministry to take time to discuss and reflect upon the following:

- Pray through the questions and ask God to help you to clarify your thinking and deepen your convictions.
- Work through the Bible references.
- Discuss the twelve marks with a trusted friend (and your spouse, if you are married).
- Be ready to be patient – God operates according to His own timetable.
- Get busy – whilst you wait make sure that you are actively involved in the ministry of a local church.
- Read some good books about ministry (see Appendix 1).
- Talk to the leaders of your church about how you feel and seek their wisdom.
- Don't give up! The qualifications and challenges of ministry may seem overwhelming – but the grace of God is more than enough to sustain you.
- Always remember that God's grace is made perfect in your weakness (2 Cor. 12:1–10).

THE PATHS INTO MINISTRY

Twenty-five years ago there was a pretty straightforward and well-trodden path into ministry training, not least because the vast majority of trainees were heading either into pastoral ministry or to the 'mission field'. Generally all that was required was to do some research, visit a few colleges and choose the course best suited to your circumstances. This was because there was a typical person suited to 'ministry', a typical route to be taken and a typical ministry open to that person (either pastorate or missionary). How times have changed – and for the better!

Today many different types of people of various ages think about ministry. Diverse ministry opportunities exist and the rise in bi-vocational ministry has opened up new possibilities for part-time ministry posts. In response to the changing scene, new and varied training options have become available.

All this has come about not just because the church has woken up to the need to invest in training but more through a recognition that in order to respond to the mission field on our own doorstep we need an array of different sorts of gospel workers. The need is for pastors, evangelists and church planters, and women's, cross-cultural, children's, youth and community workers to meet the challenge of the evangelisation of Britain and Europe today.

Over the past two and a half decades church leaders have realised that training for gospel ministry cannot be a 'one size fits all' model. Thus the range of options now on offer includes church- and college-based training; one-day and part-time courses; specialist courses; and distance and online schooling. A 'pick and mix' approach has become commonplace and the training landscape has changed out of all recognition to a quarter of a century ago.

The rise of church apprenticeship and ministry training schemes has seen church-based training take on a significant 'first call' place in exploring suitability and proven ability for training for ministry. The church has recaptured the fact that the best place to evaluate the character and gifts of a gospel worker is in the working setting of their local church. Churches and church groupings have begun to work together to provide support training for this option in many parts of the country, not least through Gospel Partnership initiatives.

Colleges have also begun to adapt to this changing scene. Today many offer access to modular or part-time courses, short-term evening classes and residential summer weeks in addition to their standard full-time residential courses. A recognition that practical leadership and pastoral skills are best learned and developed in a mentored 'on the job' setting rather than in a classroom has led to a growing willingness by colleges to invest in much closer co-operation with sending churches. Anything that provides for mentoring and training by experienced pastors, evangelists and youth workers is being encouraged.

Underlying these changes has been a recapturing of the biblical centrality of the local church as the main agent of identifying and sending out gospel workers. Increasingly the 'Lone Ranger' who embarks on gospel ministry is a thing of the past. The church as a whole – as well as colleges – have recognised that it is no longer acceptable that earnest, well-meaning but unsuitable men and women self-elect themselves to ministry, invariably bypassing the local church and its leadership en route. Today the primary role and responsibility of the local church to identify, recommend, equip and resource gospel workers from their own number has become the default position of the majority of gospel churches in the UK.

So where does this leave the man or woman who is at that stage of thinking about ministry and the ways into training? A range of options is a wonderful thing but can bring with it added agonising over which way might be best.

At this point the authors are indebted to and happy to acknowledge that the idea of coming at the question through the means of a 'ministry equation' is entirely down to Adrian Reynolds of The Proclamation Trust. We have borrowed the term, and some of the content, from a seminar entitled 'Plotting a Route into Ministry' which Adrian gave at the 2013 FIEC Hub Conference. We do so with his permission and encouragement, we are pleased to say! Here's the equation:

Who am I? + What do I need? + Where am I going? = How do I get there?

If, under God, these questions can be honestly and clearly addressed, the question of the most appropriate training and way into ministry will tend to fall into place. So let's think about each question in turn.

WHO AM I?

This is not, in this instance, a question asked in philosophical or theological terms but rather a call to **look at your own character, personality and gifting, as well as your current life and church situation**. The question flows out of a number of the twelve marks that were flagged up in 'The Call' section earlier.

2 Timothy 1:6 teaches us to think of ourselves, like Timothy, on a 'journey'. He was not the finished article but he had the essential requisite character to commend himself to the church. Unless a consistent character is in place which reflects a growing godliness, then a person ought to put aside any thoughts of ministry service until it is!

In the same epistle, Paul describes the characteristics of a gospel worker in the broadest of terms as a *'reliable'* person (2:2); as one ready to endure *'suffering'* for the cause of the gospel (2:3); and as an *'approved ... worker'* (2:15) who pursues *'righteousness, faith, love and peace'* (2:22). He concludes urging the importance of *'great patience'* and an ability to exercise *'careful instruction'* in and out of season (4:2). This catalogue of character majors upon proven dependability and humility which must be present in some significant measure.

Then there is the issue of what type of **personality** you are. Do you tend towards the extrovert or introvert end of the scale? Are you a people person who is energised by being around people or do they drain you? Are you relatively stable or do you undergo mood changes that make people wary around you? Are you able to speak the truth in love or does the prospect of confronting people scare the wits out of you? Are you easy-going or highly focused? Are you people or task orientated? None of this is to say that there is a certain 'type' suited to ministry; far from it – the Lord uses all kinds of people and personalities as part of His delightful tapestry of ministry and life. Furthermore we are all 'works in progress' and the Lord uses nothing but broken and imperfect people to do His work. But the point here is simply this: you must be self-aware and know yourself and how the Lord has wired you up as a person.

Next comes the issue of **gifting**. Be realistic about the exact nature of the gifts the Lord has given you. A young man, sensing God's call upon his life, once approached his pastors with the thought that the

Lord might be calling him to be a pastor-preacher. They were not at all surprised that he was considering ministry for he was an excellent and keen young Christian man of fine character. However, they were rather surprised at the thought that the Lord might be calling him to exercise a preaching ministry, since he had evidenced no obvious gifts in that area.

In the discussion that followed it came to light that he had only talked about 'preaching' because – and this was twenty-five years ago – it seemed to be the only route open. As a young Christian it appeared to him that this was the only real 'ministry' the church was interested in and so he had better put himself forward as a pastor-preacher. As it happened the young man was an exceptional linguist about to secure a First Class Honours degree in Linguistics and, when pressed, acknowledged that his real heart was for Bible translation! Suddenly the pastors were on board and the rest, as the saying goes, is history. After Bible college – where he met his wife! – the young man went on to spend the next twelve years translating the New Testament into the tribal language of a remote tribe in the Philippines – and today is working his way through the Old Testament for that tribe!

In other words, there should be a 'naturalness' that sees any specific ministry we aspire to matched with an evident gifting in that area. It is not unreasonable or unspiritual to expect that the gift is already being exercised in the normal course of church life.

Let's not 'super-spiritualise' in this matter of gifting. In His divine providence God makes us who we are and everyone has natural gifts and abilities. It is part of His common grace. Therefore we should not be surprised by but rather be looking out for the embryonic gifts which the Lord has given His people from birth. Gifts for ministry more often than not flow from a pre-conversion natural aptitude. It is all part of God's preparation of that person.

At the same time let's remember that in this matter of gifting the church should not be looking for the finished article! Far from it. The whole point of a gifting is that it can be constantly honed and improved. How many famous sports stars, business people and artists tell the story of how they were initially overlooked because someone failed to recognise and encourage their potential? So in Christian ministry we should look for early indications of a natural aptitude and capability since gifting is constantly a matter of progression. Paul charges the young Timothy: *'Be diligent in these matters [preaching and teaching]; give yourself wholly to them, so that everyone may see your progress'* (1 Tim. 4:15)

Never forget too that, biblically, gifting is always secondary to character. The Lord is far more interested in who we are in Him than what we do for Him.

A flawed character will eventually destroy a ministry, however gifted that person may be – and there are far too many tragic instances that litter evangelicalism in this respect. A gift can always be improved but a flawed character is cancerous.

So asking 'Who am I?' is basically a question of character and whether there is the presence of a growing godliness that must be evident in anyone considering Christian ministry of whatever kind.

Providing character and gifting are 'in place', there then follows a series of practical considerations that will help in thinking through the timing and route of any preparation and training for ministry. Some if not all of the following have to be taken into consideration and thought through:

Family situation

This is simply taking into account a person's marital status. A married person without children is generally in a place to be more flexible on the possibility of college-based training and on location thereafter. A married person with younger children has, in turn, generally more flexibility in terms of access to training and ministry location than someone whose children are in their teens. It's all about a person's age and stage of life.

Again, as a generality, single men and women have more flexibility of movement around the country –

though increasingly, for both singles and marrieds of a certain age, the issue of caring for elderly parents is becoming a factor affecting location of ministry. More and more, though, as people live longer and pensions provide some financial freedom, older people are considering a form of gospel ministry. Widows and widowers, and in some cases divorced people, are also seeking consideration for ministry. All of these present both the person and their church with particular issues over which Christians might well differ and reach opposite conclusions when it comes to eligibility.

Financial situation

The personal situation of every individual will invariably be different as will the capacity of the person and the church to help fund their training. Of course it will generally be easier for single people or those married without dependent children to have flexibility and mobility in addition to lesser financial liabilities. Access to Christian Training Trust funds might be a factor to facilitate training.

Work situation

The trend in some industries and careers to flexibility in work hours and part-time jobs provide some with the opportunity to consider training whilst still in employment. However, for the most part, a step into full-time training is the preferred option. This might be church- or college-based, or a mix of the two. Again the type of job and level of responsibility might well dictate which option is followed in respect of full- or part-time training.

A combination of circumstances regarding someone's family, financial and work situations will often make the decision regarding pursuing ministry at any given life and circumstance stage self-evident.

Home church

The support and encouragement of the home church is vital and without which – barring a few extraordinary exceptions – further training and ministry itself should rarely be countenanced. Furthermore, one would expect that the person is serving consistently and helpfully in their local church – and has been for a while. One would also look for their gift to be recognised, used and developed by the church, and a source of blessing to it.

Experience of life

Too many men and women have been encouraged into ministry in the past decade with a serious lack of life and workplace experience. In the longer term it ill-serves both them and the church they serve. In whatever ministry a person is involved in, a basic wisdom and experience in handling and leading people is vital. Ministry is both Word-based and people-focused, and we neglect either at our peril. The Bible takes very seriously the maturity, ability to lead and good reputation with non-Christians of those entrusted with the leadership of the church (1 Tim. 3:5, 7).

There must be a long-term perspective in preparing people for ministry which takes into account and promotes life and workplace experience as an integral part of suitability for ministry. Time in the workplace is not time wasted but time invested! After all, Jesus spent the greater part of His life in the workplace which, whilst not a mandate, seems to have served Him well.

Counsel of others

'Walk with the wise and become wise' says Proverbs 13:20. In our age of raging individualism, the community of God's people is a glorious and gracious provision from a Heavenly Father to guide our ways. Seek the wisdom and perspective of older men and women in the faith in both home church and other churches whom you respect and admire. In particular seek out those you know will speak what you need to hear, not what you necessarily want to hear!

Gender

FIEC churches, together with many other evangelical groupings and movements around the world, hold a 'complementarian' position on the issue of the role of male and female. Often misunderstood and misrepresented, this is not an 'anti-women' viewpoint, as is sometimes portrayed by those who do not share the position. Complementarians in fact have the highest possible view of women: they want to affirm and promote the biblical assertion that male and female are of equal worth. At the same time, though, they wish to recognise that the God-given roles of men and women are different but complementary.

When it comes to ministry roles, complementarians hold that the Bible teaches that the primary leaders and teachers of the church are to be suitably qualified men. Teaching, though, is not to be restricted to pastor, teacher or elder roles. All Christians are to be involved in teaching and encouraging one another. This includes women who are to teach other women (Tit. 2:4) and who may well be involved in teaching in other forums. How exactly this works out in practice will vary from church to church.

So the opportunities in gospel ministry are going to be different for men and women in churches holding the complementarian position. Whilst the role of pastor will be open to men only, the scope for women in ministry is still wide-ranging and embraces women's work; evangelism and cross-cultural mission to women; children's and youth ministry; administration; specialist roles in Christian agencies speaking into public life, social issues and care; as well as media and publishing ministries. The contribution of women in gospel ministry today is immense.

Age

Last but not least is the issue of age! There is no right nor wrong age to consider ministry. However, as noted above, experience of life is a very important factor in ministry, of whatever sort. The Bible also sees maturity and stability as a prerequisite of leadership (1 Tim. 3:1–7) because of the temptation, due to immaturity, of succumbing to pride (*'He must not be a recent convert, or he may become conceited and fall under the same judgment as the devil'*, 1 Tim. 3:6)

Any decision about timing for ministry has to take into account a person's stage of life. There is a balance to be struck for a younger adult between gaining some basic experience of life weighed against the opportunity their particular life stage provides with its relative freedom and mobility, which if not taken might be forfeited for many years. Much wisdom and counsel is needed and to be sought in this regard. At the same time the fact that people are living longer means that people over fifty can now think of training for and entering paid Christian ministry with a realistic expectation of twenty years of fruitful service ahead. Such a 'goals in extra time' life stage holds great potential for service and the mission of the church.

The 'Who am I?' question is the primary and most important factor to be addressed in any consideration of a path into training and ministry. Once a decision has been reached, what follows in the 'ministry equation' tends towards the pragmatic and practical issues of training and placement.

WHAT DO I NEED?

Taking as read that the person's character and gifting has the necessary proof to give confidence in encouraging them into paid gospel ministry, there are four key areas to think about:

1. Church

Explicit and implicit thus far in this consideration of a call and path into ministry has been the central place the local church will play in the process. This involvement is to be sought and expected through all the stages on the 'ministry equation' since it is the local church who are to be the prime agent in mission. It is the role of the local church leadership especially to be praying for, identifying, recognising and supporting workers for the harvest field, and their counsel and involvement is integral to this whole process. No decision, be it over suitability, training requirements and a possible placement, should be taken in isolation but rather in close consultation and under the guidance and direction of the local church leadership.

There will, sadly, be occasions where – because of the weakness or frailty of a particular local church or the absence of sufficient or adequate leadership – such support, direction and involvement will not be readily available to an individual. Where that is the case the individual should seek the help and involvement of one or more local leaders who would be able to work with that local church to provide some of this necessary help and direction.

2. Formal training

The question 'What training ought I to seek?' can be best answered with 'The best you possibly can in your circumstances'. Training is a lifetime experience and, as already noted from 1 Timothy 4:15, the call of Scripture is for Christian workers to display a discernible progression in their character and gifting. However, the initial opportunity to train is a unique one-off opportunity and thus to be used to maximum effect. For some that will mean going to a Bible college full-time for two to three years; for others a better choice will be accessing more locally available part-time options whilst training on the job in the local church. There is no 'one size fits all' answer to be had.

There is continuing debate of the pros and cons of college- versus church-based training. There are implicit strengths and weaknesses to both views and options. The cost of college-based training is considerably higher than a church-based one, and the link to an academic year means that in effect there is at most seven months of the year in direct training for those in a college setting – and often a disconnection from their home church. Critics of the college-based model point out that what could be done in two years thus takes three, with a considerable cost implication. In response, colleges point out that they do not see their main aim or role as delivering practical ministry training but rather a theological framework and foundational tools, as well as personal preparation for a lifetime of ministry.

Either way what is not in dispute is that, in recent years in Britain, the number of courses and options open to those wanting to get trained for gospel ministry has blossomed and flourished. Many men and women who, for a variety of reasons, could not previously have contemplated Bible college training have been able to access some outstanding courses and gain the support necessary to encourage their studies. In addition ministry-training day courses run by regional Gospel Partnerships throughout Britain have added to the variety of church-based training options.

Many colleges have also responded with flexibility and some ingenuity to the changing scene and needs. Most now offer some form of distance learning, access to modules or summer schools, as well as the option of taking a course a day a week over a number of years. The best colleges and training providers will particularly seek to deliver a robust theological, ministry and leadership training that understands the contemporary challenge. (A list of some of these colleges and courses can be found in Appendix 2.)

3. Informal training and mentoring

Often the most influential people in our training are those who are willing to play some kind of mentoring role. To have an older man (or woman, if we are a woman) with regular access to our lives, and us to theirs, is an invaluable means of gaining informal training and wisdom. The Apostle Paul testified to the influence Gamaliel had upon his training (Acts 22:3), which would have been in the rabbinic tradition – a model which placed huge emphasis upon learning from an older, wiser tutor and mentor. In much the same way the Lord Jesus had His disciples sit at His feet and learn.

To have a person who will not only critique your public ministry but with whom you can discuss everything from theological through to personal ministry issues is an immense benefit. It therefore ought to be sought as early as possible in any training situation.

4. Finance

Training colleges and other formal courses all cost money – and some much more than others! So part of researching options is to ascertain the course fees and, where required, accommodation costs for residential courses. Even if remaining at home in a local church-training option, there are all the usual cost-of-living expenses to be met. Whichever way is chosen there is no getting away from the fact that there is a cost involved. Increasingly many churches are willing to help those they are encouraging into ministry; indeed many rightfully see it as part of their ownership and responsibility.

There are various Christian Charitable Trusts to which students can apply for grants to help towards their theological training, and many colleges are geared up to providing details of such trusts as well as bursaries of their own.

In 2011 the FIEC set up their own training fund for churches and individuals belonging to the Fellowship and some details of this are given in the 'Here to Help' section at the close of this book.

Finally comes the third part of the first half of the 'ministry equation', namely the matter of what kind of ministry am I heading towards and training for?

WHERE AM I GOING?

This is the shortest and most easily summarised part of the equation. By the time a person has reached this stage of the process of considering ministry, they will have a clear idea of what kind of role the Lord has equipped them for and called them to.

The choice of a range of ministries

Today, as highlighted earlier, there is tremendous scope and ever-increasing opportunities and diversity in terms of ministry roles. The task of mission to a widely unevangelised nation necessitates everything from pastor-teachers, administrators and evangelists, to women's, children's, youth, family, cross-cultural and community workers plus those involved in 'seniors' ministry. In addition there are those heading overseas in fulfilment of the Great Commission of Matthew 28:19. This will include Bible translators and other specialised ministries to people groups and religions.

The option of a bi-vocational ministry

There will be places in the UK where economically it is not going to be viable to be in a fully paid position initially. The missionary challenge in Britain is a task of considerable size, and this needs to be considered together with the economics and practicalities of the situation. Therefore the use of bi-vocational ministry, whereby individuals engage in active ministry alongside other paid employment, will often be necessary as one 'stream' in any strategy the evangelical church adopts. A church that understands and promotes the place of bi-vocational as well as 'full-time' ministry is vital to the growth of the kingdom of God in the nation.

In addition there are those situations overseas where 'tent-making' is the only viable option of access into many countries who will no longer welcome missionaries in the traditional sense. To be a 'tent-maker', following the occasional practice of the Apostle Paul (Acts 18:3; 1 Thes. 2:9) is to take the opportunity that a professional or artisan qualification provides to access those same 'closed' countries. This allows 'tent-makers' to get alongside national Christians and their local churches and to support them in their evangelism and witness.

In the New Testament as well as throughout church history, bi-vocational ministry has been a significant factor in the growth of the church. Indeed, in many parts of the world today 'full-time' ministry is not an option, but that has not deterred the church from growing in a very significant way; China comes to mind by way of one example.

There are obviously limitations, pressures and challenges involved in bi-vocational ministry, not least the demands it places on families. At the same time there are compensating benefits and advantages, not least the way bi-vocational ministry automatically connects a Christian worker with the everyday world and the everyday workplace. So at the very least men and women thinking about gospel ministry ought to see bi-vocational ministry as an option to be considered, even if only for an initial period to help establish a ministry in any given area or situation.

In conjunction with practitioners and training providers, FIEC has begun to give thought to how training, equipping, support and resourcing might be provided to those men and women considering and involved in bi-vocational ministry.

A specific location?

Another factor to consider at this stage is the matter of where to minister. This is not only a matter of thinking urban or suburban, town or rural, poor or wealthy, but more especially geographically.

It is a fact that the greatest concentration of evangelical churches – and therefore financial and people resources – are in the southern part of England, not least in the so-called 'Home Counties', and in significant towns such as Bournemouth, Bristol, Birmingham and Liverpool, as well as in the province of Northern Ireland. This means that there are large tracts of England, Wales and Scotland that are, in effect, spiritual wastelands in terms of evangelical gospel witness.

The 'Go Into' research by Andy Paterson, Mission Director of FIEC, has identified fifty places in the UK in need of church planting. These are towns and significant population centres largely devoid of gospel witness. The need of the hour is for churches and those individuals the Lord is training up for the harvest field to seriously consider and commit to taking the gospel to these areas.

Which church or denomination?

This will also need to be borne in mind when choosing a training route. Whilst this book is written primarily from the perspective and expectation of those entering independent church ministry, there will be those who may well be heading for ministry within a denomination. Each denomination will have their own specific requirements for those being trained for ministry within their churches. This needs to be researched and identified before starting on a formal training course, since not all courses are going to be acceptable to varying denominations or traditions.

HOW DO I GET THERE?

Exploring and thinking through the three parts of the 'ministry equation' outlined above ought to go a long way towards answering the 'How do I get into ministry?' question that complete our 'ministry equation'.

The authors' hope and prayer is that this brief book will be used by the Lord to help you and your church think through some of the key issues surrounding this vital subject. What a joy and comfort it is to hear the familiar call and promise of Proverbs 3:6: '*in all your ways submit to him, and he will make your paths straight*'.

CONCLUSION: HERE TO HELP

For those reading this book who come from or are leaders in an FIEC church, there are two specific ways in which the Fellowship seeks to help both churches and individuals in the whole process of thinking through the call and paths into ministry:

1. THE HUB CONFERENCE

Historically, a weakness with independent churches (and this was certainly true of FIEC) lay in their very autonomy and independence, which mitigated against providing would-be gospel workers with any clear 'route into ministry'. The absence of any coherent structure or system meant that independent churches lost some of their best folk to other groups or denominations.

Churches need as much practical support and encouragement as possible as they seek to invest in training up the next generation of gospel workers. Individuals too need a network of support beyond their own church to which they can look for advice and support as they help consider and embark upon training.

The Hub Conference was launched in 2012 as an annual weekend conference bringing together those 'just thinking' about and those 'just started' upon training for Christian ministry with experienced male and female leaders from FIEC churches, as well as with representatives of college and other training course providers. Under one roof, The Hub brings all these folk together for a weekend of Bible ministry and a choice from eighteen seminars all on ministry-related issues. A key aspect is a '1-to-1' (or, in the case of a married couple, a 2-to-2) hour with one of the leadership team to discuss the particular situation those considering ministry find themselves in and to gain some wisdom and feedback – both to themselves and to their sending church.

In this manner the intention is to walk alongside both church and individual as they consider and then often commit to training for ministry. A return every year during training is encouraged, which gives a reference point outside of the local church but in support of it – again for the sake of both the church and the individual.

2. THE FIEC TRAINING FUND

In tandem with The Hub Conference, access to the FIEC Training Fund is available to those from FIEC churches. Often the financial resources of both individuals and local churches is stretched and acts as a serious barrier to a person receiving the in-depth theological and practical training necessary for a lifetime of ministry. Therefore the Training Fund seeks to promote and support the development of suitably gifted men and women by two prime areas of investment:

(a) to assist FIEC churches to create training posts for gospel workers
(b) to assist individuals access training for gospel ministry

The maximum grant awarded to a church is currently £15,000 p.a. and to an individual £7,500 p.a., and this is normally awarded for two consecutive years. The weighting in favour of churches reflects an awareness that a church is largely dependent upon itself for raising funds whereas an individual has several potential sources of support to draw upon (for example, their church, family and friends, other grant-making bodies and their own savings). Furthermore, in making larger grants to churches, the intention is to encourage churches to create new posts to develop gospel ministry in their locality whilst at the same time helping individuals who have completed initial training to find a job – which has been a significant issue for many in the past.

A FINAL WORD

As stated at the outset, this is not a definitive or exhaustive guide to the call and paths into ministry, but we do hope that the principles and practices highlighted here will act as a stimulus and guide to enable you, whether an individual or a church leader, to begin to negotiate a journey that is both daunting and thrilling.

There is no set route the Lord uses to draw workers into His harvest field. There are, however, some timeless truths and biblical wisdom which we trust this short book has reflected and contributed towards.

NOTES

1. Some writers are uncomfortable with the concept of 'feeling a call' from God, dismissing it as 'the language of pietism' – see, for example, *Do You Feel Called by God?* by Michael Bennett (Matthias Media, 2012). The intention behind this objection is that pietism can lead to a very subjective and unbiblical longing for some kind of life-transforming experience, without which no one should consider ministry. I agree that this is unhelpful. However, I think that it is an overreaction. We cannot depend on internal impressions alone, but there must be a measure of inner conviction based on a careful examination of clear biblical criteria before we contemplate pastoral ministry.
2. Richard Baxter, *The Reformed Pastor* (Multnomah, 1982), p. 3.
3. Charles H. Spurgeon, *Lectures to My Students* (Marshall, Morgan & Scott, 1982), pp. 9–10.
4. Richard Baxter, *The Reformed Pastor*, p. 69.
5. Kevin DeYoung, *Don't Call It a Comeback* (Crossway, 2011), p. 26.
6. Alistair Begg, *'The Pulpit: Its Power and Pitfalls'* (a lecture at the Whitefield Ministerial Fraternal, Wheaton, Illinois, 1993).
7. Charles Bridges, *The Christian Ministry* (The Banner of Truth Trust, 1830), p. 91.
8. Charles H. Spurgeon, *Lectures to My Students*, p. 29.

APPENDIX 1

RECOMMENDED BOOKS AND ARTICLES

The Art and Practice of Bivocational Ministry
Dennis Bickers (Beacon Hill Press, 2013).

Going the Distance
Peter Brain (Matthias Press, 2004).

Gospel DNA
Richard Coekin (Co-Mission, 2013).

Preparation for Ministry
Allan Harman (Banner of Truth, 2015).

Fruitful Leaders
Marcus Honeysett (IVP, 2011).

Brothers, We Are Not Professionals
John Piper (Christian Focus Publications, 2008; updated and expanded edition Broadman & Holman Publishers, 2013).

A Christian Guide to Leadership
Derek Prime (Evangelical Press, 2005).

Lectures to My Students
C.H. Spurgeon (Banner of Truth, 2008).

On Being a Servant of God
Warren Wiersbe (10Publishing, 2015).

For a helpful article on the FIEC's position on the role of women in the church, see:
fiec.org.uk/resources/article/women-in-ministry-statement

APPENDIX 2

COLLEGES AND COURSES

Cornhill Training Course
140–148 Borough High Street, London SE1 1LB
T: 020 7407 0562
www.proctrust.org.uk/cornhill

Edinburgh Theological Seminary (ETS)
15 North Bank Street, The Mound, Edinburgh EH1 2LS
T: 0131 226 5286
www.ets.ac.uk

London Theological Seminary
104 Hendon Lane, London N3 3SQ
T: 020 8346 7587
www.ltslondon.org

Moorlands College
Sopley, Christchurch, Dorset BH23 7AT
T: 01425 674500
www.moorlands.ac.uk

Oak Hill College
Chase Side, Southgate, London N14 4PS
T: 020 8449 0467
www.oakhill.ac.uk

Porterbrook
2 Boyer Street, Loughborough LE11 1DT
T: 0114 267 6704
porterbrooknetwork.org

School of Missional Discipleship
69 Above Bar Street, Southampton SO14 7FE
T: 023 8022 8275
abovebarchurch.org.uk/serve/school-of-missional-disciple-making

Third Millennium Ministries
316 Live Oaks Boulevard, Casselberry, FL 32707, USA
T: 407.830.0222
thirdmill.org

Union
Bryntirion House, Bridgend CF31 4DX
T: 01656 645411
www.west.org.uk/union

Urban Ministries
email: getintouch@urbanministries.org.uk
www.urbanministries.org.uk

WEST (Wales Evangelical School of Theology)
Bryntirion House, Bridgend CF31 4DX
T: 01656 645411
www.west.org.uk

Trevor Archer and Paul Mallard
THE CALL
SERIES EDITORS: Trevor Archer and Dan Green
fiec